75 Years

A Woman's Life in Verse

75 Years

A Woman's Life in Verse

by

Michelle Koubek

© 2025 Michelle Koubek. All rights reserved.
This material may not be reproduced in any form, published,
reprinted, recorded, performed, broadcast,
rewritten or redistributed without
the explicit permission of Michelle Koubek.
All such actions are strictly prohibited by law.

Cover design by Shay Culligan
Cover image by Kamil Ślusarczyk on Unsplash
Author photo by Michelle Koubek

ISBN: 978-1-63980-842-7

Kelsay Books
502 South 1040 East, A-119
American Fork, Utah 84003
Kelsaybooks.com

*for my parents for teaching me to believe in myself,
and my husband, Kyle, for always believing in me*

Acknowledgments

I am full of gratitude to all of the people who have contributed their stories, indirectly or directly, to this collection of poems to make it an authentic representation of a woman's life from the earliest moments into the twilight years.

Thank you to the women of the International Women's Writing Guild for providing me with a haven for my passion. Thank you for your generations of experiences that have inspired many of these poems.

Thank you to the women—friends, family, professionals, and acquaintances—that shall remain anonymous but who have shared their stories and wisdom with me.

Thank you to my teachers that encouraged me to keep writing from elementary school through college. I wouldn't have ever thought I could do something like this without your lessons.

Thank you to my poppy, George Strouse. Your passion for the arts and knowledge has always made you a role model to me. Thank you to my late nan, Lillian Strouse. You showed me how fierce a woman can be.

Thank you to my late grandpa, Harry Frett Jr., for instilling resilient joy in my being. Thank you to my late grandmother, Marie Frett, for showing me that a sharp mind and warm heart can go hand-in-hand.

Thank you to my dad, David Frett, for his consistent words of wisdom and inspiring me to be brave in the face of uncertainty.

Thank you to my mom, Debra Frett, for passing on her creative spirit and always nurturing me so that I could reach for my dreams.

As for my husband, Kyle Koubek, your patience and unyielding support are priceless. Only you know the true extent of the sacrifices that have been made for compiling this collection. I will never be able to repay you for what you do for me every day. I love you with all my heart.

Contents

I. The First Twenty-Five

Zero	15
One	16
Two	17
Three	18
Four	19
Five	20
Six	21
Seven	22
Eight	23
Nine	24
Ten	25
Eleven	26
Twelve	27
Thirteen	28
Fourteen	29
Fifteen	30
Sixteen	31
Seventeen	32
Eighteen	33
Nineteen	34
Twenty	35
Twenty-One	36
Twenty-Two	37
Twenty-Three	38
Twenty-Four	39
Twenty-Five	40

II. The Twenty-Five in Between

Twenty-Six	43
Twenty-Seven	44
Twenty-Eight	45
Twenty-Nine	46
Thirty	47
Thirty-One	48
Thirty-Two	49
Thirty-Three	50
Thirty-Four	51
Thirty-Five	52
Thirty-Six	53
Thirty-Seven	54
Thirty-Eight	55
Thirty-Nine	56
Forty	57
Forty-One	58
Forty-Two	59
Forty-Three	60
Forty-Four	61
Forty-Five	62
Forty-Six	63
Forty-Seven	64
Forty-Eight	65
Forty-Nine	66
Fifty	67

III. The Last Twenty-Five

Fifty-One	71
Fifty-Two	72
Fifty-Three	73
Fifty-Four	74
Fifty-Five	75
Fifty-Six	76
Fifty-Seven	77
Fifty-Eight	78
Fifty-Nine	79
Sixty	80
Sixty-One	81
Sixty-Two	82
Sixty-Three	83
Sixty-Four	84
Sixty-Five	85
Sixty-Six	86
Sixty-Seven	87
Sixty-Eight	88
Sixty-Nine	89
Seventy	90
Seventy-One	91
Seventy-Two	92
Seventy-Three	93
Seventy-Four	94
Seventy-Five	95

I. The First Twenty-Five

Zero

In the beginning, I cry.
Too young to have dreams, so hunger will do,
and so begins my eternal conflict with the pit.

Netted by the noises around me,
tangling me into confusion
with laughing lights above that are entertained
by my extinguishable light,
a soul seeking purpose,

and as I wail louder, angry at the crowded void I have entered,
time is a breath between cries,
until warm arms like days guide me to safety—
my mother's face.

There is hope in the chaos.

One

Stand
like the tallest elm untruncated by time,
the greatest tower that proves the hours,
the person you will become.
Step
like a warrior—unworn by war,
a queen towards her throne of tolerance not tyranny,
a child who knows where she must go.
Fall
like Rome,
the Library of Alexandria,
something that can only hope to be great forever.

Consider if it's worth getting up
only to fall eventually.

Stand anyway.

Two

I want that, too, just like Brother,
I want to try that sweet pink stuff, too.

I want you to hold me, too, I want
you to protect me, too,

I want,
I want,
I want, too.

I want to be heard when I scream, too, I want to
be special, too, I want

Daddy to tell me the story, too, with that
same funny voice like a cranky clown.

I want,
I want,
I want, too.

Such is the terrible too's.

Three

That four-legged animal is a horse that
could also be a zebra,
while that animal with wings could be a duck
or a chicken.

Mommy's mommy and Daddy's daddy, but
that man with the big head is sometimes called
Bobby or uncle.

I have to eat my vegetables, even when I don't know
their names, and I prefer to call them all, YUCK,

while *no* is still my favorite, although
it doesn't always seem to work,

but at least I know what the sweet pink stuff is now, so
maybe learning words isn't the worst.

It's *bubblegrum ice scream,* by the way.

Four

Looking out the fence of the schoolyard for Mother to arrive,

looking out the fence of the schoolyard for Mother to arrive,

looking out the fence of the schoolyard for Mother to arrive,

looking, looking, looking out the—Tag! I'm it?

Five more minutes, please, Mom!

Five

Monarch butterflies are kings and
queens, while chrysalises are Baroque bedrooms.

A giant sleepover that lasts for few weeks in
the chattering cage of my classroom as

the cage of soon-to-be royalty sleeps.
A flash of bittersweet honey wings framed by

black piping, and we, the courtiers of
kindergarten, cheer.

The kings and queens finally awake, reminding
us of our place in the world.

Six

I am going to start today by impressing you, Teacher.
Plank for a back, duct tape lips,
you won't hear me or see me unless you want to

but if you choose to, I'll be sparkling like
that plaque above your door that reads
Reach for your dreams,

and now you're reviewing the alphabet, I
know all about that.
A question?
I know the answer. Please, call on me, Teacher.
No, don't look at him!
Shout out the answer with a shuddering scream,
yet you scowl.

So, that wasn't correct? Oh, the answer
was right, but
it's me that's wrong.
Tried my best to impress you,
but all I got was

ten minutes off recess, Ana,
and
I'm calling your mom.

Seven

Today I'm going to show myself to you
and hope that you don't tell me I'm worthless.
Your reaction could launch me into the opera of outer space,
so I never come down, or I'll combust on
the launchpad that is elementary school.

I've spent three days working on this drawing
of a species-less tree with a dramatically orange bird in it
because I really want to know what you think.
Is it good? Don't lie to me.

You're holding it upside down.

Eight

In my backyard, tiger caterpillars that
I let prowl on the promontory of my
hand.

Speak to them, tiny tickles, tickles,
tickles of brushing paws on my skin.

Ask if they will be safe in the
jungle of treetop grass blades, and
I'm told *not to worry* as the yardwork
begins.

In my backyard, the remains of dozens of
tiger caterpillars, reminding me of the
chaos I thought I'd conquered.

I growl in fury.

Nine

Eleanor and I take pictures in my parent's bathroom
because we want to feel sophisticated.
Ten necklaces too many, rouged cheeks like Cortland apples,
courting ourselves by posing like the magazine girls.
Before washing our faces and
putting on pjs to watch
whatever Mom picked up from Blockbuster.
And as we laugh, overheating like logs in our sleeping bags
that are meant for camping outside,
our cheeks are red like Cortland apples once more,
but we don't think to photograph it,
Eleanor and I.

Ten

Get on the bus. Keep my head down.
Don't stick out   too far.

Find my classroom. Stay in my seat.
Don't let my chair stick out   too far.

I discover the graffiti on the wall
of the girl's bathroom that
declares, "bois smel,"

before I add my own masterpiece,
a toucan who gives the illusion of
hopping from soap dispenser to dispenser.

Go back to class. Find my desk. Stay in my seat.
Don't stick out   too far.

Eleven

Never had a fear of numbers.
Never had a fear of the nurse.
Never had a fear of midday moves out of class.
Never had a fear of stepping onto the scale with my shoes.

Until the nurse said that number,
the one that was ten, twenty, more than the rest.
Ever since, I quake at all four,
because my number was *just a little too large.*

Twelve

Homeroom doesn't feel like home,
especially when the room is homogenous. How can
I fit when they all drip with confidence
like stalactites?

                                    Maybe it would be better if this was
                        a cave, and I could roost in a dark corner
with stalagmites of textbooks creating my own chamber.

But instead, I sit, lost in the
shadows of oozy peers, and question
why I'm still dry as a
fossil.

Thirteen

Trying on faces,
trying on moods,
exchanging coyness for cringeworthy courage,
wearing *those* rainbow jeans.

A dressing room for womanhood,
attempting to reveal just enough of myself to be cool,
sinking into the synchrony with others who came before,
and then, there's you, Eleanor.

You hate the dressing room,
only liking it when it was pretend.
You'd rather be climbing trees, and I want to stay in your world,
so I climb.

Halfway up,
almost to you,
not long now.

Then, I forget how to play.

I return to the dressing room, that prismatic prison—this time,
locking the door.

Fourteen

Fourteen descriptions of fourteen.

Pizza with cheesy tentacles.
Prank calls on popcorn painted floors.
Flashlight tag turmoil.
Coffee with three sugar cubes.
Eggplant dress (delete all those pictures, Mom)
Blueberry water ice tongues.
Silly string pasta in my hair.
That's fine. Just be safe.
Soccer try-outs.
Broken arm, broken hopes.
Page-turning ballads under blanket forts.
Mom's old denim jacket.
Repainting my room like Da Vinci.

The best.

Fifteen

Dancing in my bedroom to (   )
while the cd of (   ) rots in my bottom drawer
because (   ) isn't popular in ninth grade.

Styling my hair in a (   )
like (   ) did in that movie,
then messing it up,
because I don't quite look the part.

Writing (   )'s name over and over again in my journal
which is locked, but (   ) has a spare key.

Trying to get some sleep, except I'm too nervous about tomorrow.
Ms. (   ) is announcing our (   ).

Sixteen

I've had crushes before but this crush is not a crush,
it's a squeeze.
A squeeze around my chest, every day, so I can't speak,
blue reckless eyes, even more reckless words,
I've never felt so compelled to be a desk,
or a wall,
or a locker,
so He won't expect me to talk back.
And He can't like me,
because I'm not like the girls that He goes for,
just as He knows I should be with someone more restrained,
but I see how He turns towards me when I pass—
just before I look away.

Seventeen

One state away is far enough to be a canyon,
but one with a bridge. While seven states away
is another planet with aliens that look (sort of) like me.
And in-state is like taking a stroll outside my childhood
home, and leaving the front door open.
But if I only go for a walk, will I ever learn how to sprint to my destination?

A medium-sized campus is big enough to be a lake,
but one with boats on it. While a large campus
is a flood with lots of unearthed secrets.
And a small campus is like taking a
bath, and leaving the window cracked open.
But if I stay in my childhood tub, will I ever learn how to swim in the sea?

What's the right way to live?

Make a decision, they say.
It's only everything.

Eighteen

Princess curtains, gauzy as purple creeks, frame my
sanctuary.

A stash of skittles in the closet,
multi-colored mischief after midnight.

Bottom bunk, top-minded, and hours
wedged between laughter like lost hair ties
on the side of my bed.

Microwave mayhem,
bedroom banquets,
hallway hikes,
Sunday grease-soaked sandwiches.

Just a sip, just a kiss,
just a hundred nights
to always remember.

Nineteen

I'm not going to beg you to be my friend,
but you will make a beggar of me.
Perfectly done bronzer with the appearance of blending,
when really the distinction is clear between you and me.
You stay in your parapets and toss ropes down as you please,
while I, a peasant, will grab the wrong lifeline
and crash.
I won't beg you to be my friend,
but please, tell me something:

Why did you pretend to be one?

Twenty

A party for every temperament
like pantyhose for any shade of skin.
Some are wild, with snags in their linings,
some are like dives into silky bliss via too much Everclear and
    juice.

Some are subtle, so the neighbors question if it's a party or a get
    together,
while some you'd rather toss in the bin, and
some are natural, so you forget where you are and let your eyeliner
become tire treads, which helps you ignore how
some compress the air out of you,
so you forget how to speak as unwelcome hands take the
    pantyhose off.
But mostly,
the parties are good.

Twenty-One

Jessica is never particularly clever,
particularly pretty,
or particularly anything
other than particularly particular.
Jessica always drinks the same whipped Pinnacle vodka,
attends even the boring classes,
and gets poppy seed bagels from the café with low fat cream
    cheese
before studying in a meeting room surrounded by people in shared
    suffering.
Jessica is obsessed with Selena Gomez,
has watched every episode of Friends no less than three times,
wants to graduate to work at her father's realty business as a
    bookkeeper,
and loves the wok in the college cafeteria.
Jessica is my best friend through freshmen freedom to senior
    sobriety.
With her, I can just be Ana.

Twenty-Two

Regret waterfalls over my fingers,
dripping, dripping between the cracks like a meadow in
a kaleidoscope. Impossible tragedy,
as inevitable as Jessica no longer replying to my texts,
but I never saw that coming either.
How many glossy grins, ultramarine upsets, cadmium orange raves
lie in the melting scene?

If only someone had warned me that
college is making a painting,
and adulthood is catching the colors
before they flee.

Twenty-Three

But then, there's order,
purpose,
order in purpose.
A uniform to belong,
bearing the same cloth though we come from different ones,
material that makes our bonds more than immaterial.

Common goals,
uncommon dreams,
there is more to these men and women
than a slip of white paper saying good job.
These people have stories,
these people are legendary,
these people are and always will be the arms that raise me.

And how is it that I belong here more than anywhere
even when I don't talk much,
lash out like a whip,
and can't hold my liquor?

We could be family if I give this a chance—
but what are the chances of that happening?

Twenty-Four

His name is Joshua, and he has flee-to-the-forest eyes.
Carefully honest, passionate in pursuit,
like a beachcomber sorting through the broken shells that might cut.

I fall into him,
forgetting to fall in,
and then,
      fall,
            fall,
                  fall.

But he's good with his manner,
and croons off-key to me at night,
so, he becomes what I want him to be:

a new life.

Twenty-Five

Love is
putting the toilet seat down daintily,
bringing the groceries in from the Honda without rushing,
making a late-night visit to McDonald's for nuggets with a smile.

But love is also
taking care of your dental health—gingivitis is serious!
Admitting defeat for that fight you clearly won.
Telling them when their tanning lotion has streaks (don't let me go outside like that!)

Joshua is
all of those things,
and when he's not, he learns.

Sometimes, we are perfect.
Always, we're close.

II. The Twenty-Five in Between

Twenty-Six

I won't be forgetting this day for a while.

Old,
new,
borrowed,
blue,
I walk down the aisle.

Yet also

sweating,
clumsy,
heels,
flash photography,
I trip.

I was right.

I won't be forgetting this day for a while.

Twenty-Seven

Kyra is a sandstorm of a yellow lab who likes to chew wood.

Kyra is in big trouble because she was supposed to be good.

But Kyra doesn't like to be left alone,

and Joshua is a proud new daddy.

So, Kyra sleeps in bed with us

like nothing ever happened.

Twenty-Eight

Joshua says, "let's try,"
and there's no going back to shore.
But we're excited by the possibility of minor rapids,
so we allow ourselves to be submerged.
While I proofread articles for the county paper,
and learn to handle the rip currents before the water
becomes inevitably rough.
I can't stop thinking of cradles and word docs,
dreaming in nursery rhymes sung by mermaids with
bubbles in their tangled hair, which is all
so wonderful, that sometimes I don't
even fight the river we're in.
Instead, I float.

Twenty-Nine

Hanna calls me in the middle of a whirlpool of
approaching deadlines and weeping mornings,
and plucks me out.
Talks to me like we're close friends,
instead of two co-workers working close.
Lets me be someone for a while,
the person that guides the river as opposed to riding it.
Lets me be hopeful, each day, that she'll call again,
and then, she does.

So, as I toss another failed test in the trash,
I still feel important.

Thirty

My cousin, Tiffany, has her first baby at twenty-three.

Thirty-One

When Hanna switches jobs, I fall back into the water.

No baby because no one knows why,
so I wish the river would swallow me.

But still, Joshua,
always Joshua,
this time, in line at the liquor store.

Joshua lugs the bottle of Captain Morgan home like a
buoy that's really a tombstone
and lays it in front of me.

I don't want to die, but what am I living for?
I take off my life vest.

Thirty-Two

All around me, sea monsters.

Thirty-Three

Crawling out of the monstrous mouth that has eaten me
doesn't leave me less digested.
Parts are missing—like that middle finger I used to wag at
danger—and my legs are too weak to stand
without Joshua supporting me.
It quickly feels like trading one blade for another,
except one is dull and one is sharp.
Yet the days become months and the months become longer
until someone cuts me off on I-90,
and I hold my arm out the window,
realizing my middle finger's grown back
while my soul was healing.

Thirty-Four

Thirty-four is like being backstage at a concert you don't care
about seeing.

I understand the skills it requires, the mechanics of it all now,
but still, I'd rather be at a Beastie Boys concert than Celine Dion.

So, Joshua and I do what we can with our VIP passes,
which are really the untouched savings we have in the bank.

We use them to hang up posters,
buy a stellar sound system,
and then rock out in our roll

downhill

at as many off-the-beaten path restaurants we can.

But this time the slope leads to bliss,
and I like the band.

Thirty-Five

If I could build a moment, it would be like this. Sun-blessed skin, wind-weary ponytail, the sound of ice clinking like polished crystal. Nothing to do, but everything to be done, and plenty of time to get doing. A retreat shoreside underneath canoodling clouds that leaves me uninterested in getting away, and every time sunglass strangers look at me, I see myself in their plastic eyes. It's as though I uncover who I should be with each step I take in the sand.

And then, an idea comes.

Thirty-Six

Eight years old but *ain't that little!* We adopt a child named Maisie.

Thirty-Seven

Like Joshua, Maisie loves to run.
Patters in the kitchen at 7 am
become my alarm.
Pitter-patter, pitter-patter, pat, pat, pat!
That would be Maisie dancing towards the backdoor,
followed by a throaty laugh as Joshua follows her.

I could get up, but I won't
because there's no rush when the house is empty.
Not that it ever feels like the void anymore.
Instead—as if our home has welcomed thousands of bumblebees—
it's always buzzing.

And as I lie there in my hive,
I'm a queen for the first time in my existence.
Even as Kyra jumps on the bed, licking my face,
I note her yellow fur and picture her with glorious wings
just like the rest of us.

Thirty-Eight

Of all the sums I've added, and all
the differences I've found,
I cannot say that any have ever given me more loss
than the ones that left me in the positive, so I
should be okay, but I'm not,
because one is sometimes more.

1+1+1+1-1= 3

We bury Kyra next to the toolshed.

Thirty-Nine

Gray is black and white in conflict,
as if anything comprehensible can come out of war.

Gray is moral ambiguity like a blurred line in
the sand viewed from above.

Gray is that stepping stone leading to nowhere
because we never had the patience to make more.

And I've been wondering a lot lately as I grimace at my graying
hair:

Why do we become grayer with age as if
we aren't sure what we stand for when
wisdom is supposed to follow more years?

Forty

Soprano floorboards tell me that Joshua has arrived home with
    Maisie,
but the song is discordant.

Shoulders like mountains rise and fall as Maisie hunches on the
    sofa.

Tears orate a story of growing up,
lost friends lining lost hopes,
one, specifically, Maisie never thought to not have.

Yet there's her report card—straight A's again—
buried in the bottom of her bookbag in its insignificance
as if it's a pebble instead of a gem.

And I think about how I never appreciated my potential either.

I'm going back to school.

Forty-One

The dream when I was younger,
a jar of ladyfingers atop the fridge.
The intention,
reaching for it.
And when I'm too short,
wait until someone comes,
hoping that they hand it to me.

The dream now,
the same jar of ladyfingers in the same place.
The intention,
living for it.
But at this age, I take everything out of the fridge,
stacking to form a stairway to the top,
so I can no longer wait to get there,
or else I will starve to death.

Forty-Two

Every day, I'm working to become a teacher.
I'm writing essays in between driving Maisie to softball.
I'm constructing comments in reply to my classmates.
I'm trying my best to show myself I'm still capable.

While also burning the meatloaf because I got a C instead of an A
and telling Joshua I'm tired when he's frisky before bed and
slamming the laptop too hard when I can't figure out the answer
    and
misplacing the reading glasses on my head

and messaging my professor cordially while crying and
calculating how much money we'd lose if I withdrew in this
    moment and
begging Joshua to tell me to stop,
but he's too supportive.

He'll never let me give up.

If all of us survive this,
I'll have to remember to thank him for that.

Forty-Three

Snobby blank notebooks and pompous pencils with
perfect points, desks arranged in lines without disorder,
lesson plans that haven't been tested, books
that haven't been read, a calendar of
Velcro numbers, a wall of awards without
awardees, cubbies for little human cubs,
snacks so they don't turn into hibernating bears,
and my name in bubble letters on the board,
the most satisfying prize:
Mrs. Philips.

Forty-Four

Maisie's sweet sixteen,
my mother's semi-sour sixty-fifth,
Maisie's first date,
my mother's last clean plate,
Maisie's learning to drive,
my mother's forgetting her address,
Maisie's asking for advice on *that* boy with *that* face,
my mother's asking for help with prescriptions,
Maisie's thinking about dyeing her hair,
my mother's thinking about dying,
I go back and forth between the two,
hoping all of me doesn't spill out—
the sauce of this domestic sandwich.

Forty-Five

There's nothing I can do about it
when I meet my ghost.

She's attached herself to me, and now
even when I don't see her,
she's there,
haunting every activity with blurry boos.

I wish that I could cleanse her away,
and to an extent I can,

but they warn that she'll always be waiting if
I don't swallow my white-and-blue pride.

So, this is what it's like to have hypertension.

Forty-Six

Joshua's trading his twenty-four years as a tradesman
for a boat with a hole in it.

Joshua's found his old touch-me jeans in his dresser
and is convinced the supermarket cashier is flirting with him.

Joshua's asking me if he's still got it as he looks at his threadbare head,
and he doesn't believe me when I say he does.

But at least Joshua is working out now.
Plus, I've always loved a man in a baseball cap.

Forty-Seven

And suddenly, the hostel of hostas at the
hardware store looks lonely,
so I buy a truckload of them like some kind of a heroine.

I take them home, and harbor them in our front yard,
petting their tops like they're human.

Before playing Gregory Porter for them, which they swoon over
with bent leaf heads, and talking to them about
their future in our garden.

Joshua teases me saying I'm empty nesting
since Maisie's at college

but that's not what I'm doing,

is it?

Forty-Eight

cracking,
snapping,
wandering,
waking up in sweaty storms before sun up

speechless,
SCREAMING,
questioning,
    no reply
        no reply
            no reply

breathing out and collapsing in,
the void could retake me

she was my hope in the beginning amid the chaos,

Mother,

I wasn't ready to lose you yet.

Forty-Nine

Some conclusions are carousels
that you have to time your jump off of.
Some conclusions are trampolines
that propel you higher than you've ever been.
Some conclusions are escalators
that always had a fixed end.
Losing my mother was an escalator that I couldn't
see the summit of, but when I stop teaching,
it's a little of all three, and more like
jumping from a moving vehicle
than a low-speed ride,

so I throw myself off into Joshua's waiting arms
like he's my air bag to make the impact
less shattering.

Fifty

I don't care what you think anymore.
I'm a fortress.
Load up your cannons and cock your pistols,
nothing will get through.
Just don't smile as you stand by my gates
and don't compliment what I've done with my moat
like you're not the enemy.
If you're too nice,
I'll surely believe you,
and this, my fortress that repels all
pain, will be all for nothing.

III. The Last Twenty-Five

Fifty-One

The road is a gray bullet that will kill me if I stop.
Three months on wheels,
coast-to-coast and what's in between,
it still heats me up as we ride that bullet to places we've never been.
In Illinois, I'm tired.
In Nebraska, I am brave.
In Utah, I'm curious.
In California, I'm unhinged.
In Texas, I am rowdy.
In Louisiana, I am cool.
In Florida, I am sunburnt.
In North Carolina, I'm old hiking boots.
In Maryland, I'm dreaming.
In Maine, I'm awake.
In New York, I'm living.
In Pennsylvania, I'm back.

Fifty-Two

So, that's it, then.
The show's at its finale
in the final week of May in my fifty-second year.

No more monthly tango,
dips in my mood,
no more waltzes to the pharmacy at 7 am.

A conclusion to quicksteps to the bathroom,
jiving with Joshua over words that sound
out of pitch around this time.

A closing bow to the flamenco of
evading white pants and swimsuits.

Roses in the form of a doctor's note,
scribbling off what's done is done.

I'm not a dancer anymore.
I'm a part of the audience.

But mostly, I feel *thank God.*

Fifty-Three

Maisie tiptoes around what she has to tell me
like the words are made of water
and she fears she'll drown if too much comes out.
I stay dry, listening as a good mother should,
while wringing my hands into ruin—
two scaly fish rubbed to the bone.
She's fussing with the edges of her sleeve,
hiding her hands in the fabric like a seal
as she always does when she thinks we're about to argue.
I know what I have to do.
Just a little nudge towards the edge and

she swan dives into the truth.

A moment of panic before I ask, "Why so soon?"
To which she replies, "Life is short."

Fifty-Four

Maisie's moved out to live with her new husband, Graham,
so it's suddenly only Joshua and me in the hive.
We still fly about, but there's less buzzing,
and so much honey that sometimes my stomach heaves.
Then, a new discovery, whenever we turn our backs on each other
there are our stingers.
Joshua tries to snap his off, but I embrace mine,
stinging him over and over and over again
like I hate him,

but I don't think I do,
not really.

Fifty-Five

Memory is a sieve at my age, which makes me grateful I took so
many photos.
Regardless, there are details that never slip away,
almost enlarged by the loss of others.
Joshua, in particular, clings to his memory of me saying I love
squirrels—once.
Squirrel hand towels,
squirrel blankets,
squirrel salt-and-pepper shakers,
our hive is becoming a forest.

But I smile each time he hands me another,
because he's my favorite nut.

Fifty-Six

And there it goes, my sanity, coasting away in the breeze,
like a pennant released from its stake.

I never thought I would need to safeguard my
sanity as if it could soar away,
but if I don't find something to do fast, I'll
find myself lost.

So, I chase it down, leap to grab it, and hold it close.

After that, I weave my sanity into my cross-stitching and bake
it into that new recipe for cinnamon croissants,
praying that it will never flee again
if I just stay busy enough.

Fifty-Seven

For every person that gazes up at the blue sky seeing endless possibilities,
there's another person who only sees a barrier.
Nothing but blue—tranquil and subtle—
just like a hospital gown being tugged over your naked body.
And how far can we really expect to go
when our backs are exposed,
and beyond the blue is darkness?
That's what I think about when Joshua's admitted to the hospital for his heart attack,
and they tell me it will be months before he can run again.

Then, I think of our house and realize it might not be a hive or a forest at all.

It may be a coffin.

Fifty-Eight

Did hope really die with my mother?

Fifty-Nine

Imbibed inheritance—sometimes, I worry about Maisie.
Bubbly like champagne, her essence is extraverted,
inhibition in her limbs like liquor

and her mouth is a corkscrew that can
open up any poor soul down to their
core

while her celebrations are unrestrained, a
wine glass with a fragile stem who
doesn't realize she's on the edge before she
slips.

Then, Maisie tells me she's pregnant.

There it is.

Hope is back.

Sixty

Maisie needs me more than ever, so
like a fountain I pour my love into her and my new granddaughter,
Caroline.

Gushing at the blessings I have,
overflowing as I watch baby milestones,

like learning to stand, falling and getting back up
just like we all did at her age.

Except Caroline treats it like it's never been
done before by making the most
help me face I've ever seen.

I wonder if she realizes how we all
once hoped to be great,
as she gets back up,
wibble wobbles, wibble wobbles,
then steadies and makes me believe.

Sixty-One

Using Caroline as an excuse to go to the beach,
because I haven't been there this year.
Buying Caroline sunglasses with dopey dolphins on them,
then taking her to the pier.

Pointing out the seagulls and naming them,
so she can go home and tell Maisie.
Holding up a French fry to get the seagull *real close*—
I shriek as it swoops down.

She laughs like Mother did.

Sixty-Two

Summer is over
beyond the sum of its parts
Joshua has died.

Sixty-Three

Joshua.

Sixty-Four

Joshua.

Sixty-Five

Joshua.

Sixty-Six

Sat for three hours today watching larks in the oak of my backyard,
so I guess I'm now a birdwatcher.
Singing, singing, what do they have to sing about?
Do they know something I don't?
It's a clash of notes until there's a flash
of red wing against blue sky.
You could say it's like blood,
or you could call it a ribbon
tying us together as one of the larks flies so high up
it enters the heavens.

Sixty-Seven

I didn't expect to see you here in this
grey-bearded gymnasium that we used to
giggle in as girls, but if I've learned anything,
it's that life is a steady surprise, not a jump scare.

You seem shocked that I recognize you, too,
between your trail-marked face that promotes
all your adventures,
and your hot pink hair that makes you look
like a Troll doll down to your unsanctimonious smile.

Yet there's people you forget and people
you don't, because they're the fluff
that makes your life interesting and worth
biting into.

I didn't expect to ever see you again.

How have you been, Eleanor?

Sixty-Eight

Like a charm, Eleanor's been married three times
to perfectly charming men that charmed their
way into snake pits. The problem is,
Eleanor always realized too late that
was just them shedding their skin to
reveal they were serpents.

So, Eleanor has sprouted fangs herself, and
likes to hiss when *kids these days* toss
footballs too close to her Ford

but she's also great fun, jade-green eyes
ever shimmering, and we spend more days
than I can tally pretending to be kids again.

The only difference is now, when we watch movies
together, she hisses,
clossssed captssssioning.

Sixty-Nine

2 Down: The O in OMDB
Today I'm OVER crossword puzzles.

Seventy

Joshua would have hated that joke.

Seventy-One

Seeing Eleanor and Maisie side-by-side is
sun in winter. Two glowing women, brilliant
and resilient, reminding me of dancing to (   )
in my bedroom at fifteen,
when I thought I could be like that

and maybe I have been, in some years, a
sun that didn't emulate a moon, occasionally letting
everyone circle her.

Joshua would tell me I was always the center of everything,
but now it's Maisie and Eleanor and, if all goes well, Caroline

one day.

I soak in the starlight.

Seventy-Two

Like a final impatient scratch as the first
wound heals, this tears me open again.

I didn't know what you hid, and
perhaps, it served me right, when
I never revealed why I abandoned you
years ago.

Yet the pain is no less a pirate
that loots my spirit of the riches that
are left. I've been plundered again
and again, in a ship aptly named
Life,
and your end makes me think about mine.

But at least, your daughters and sons mix
you in with the trees. You'll start at the roots, then eventually,
climb towards the lying sky.

It would be good if you could inject it with
a bit of you, letting it feel your disease,

yet if you can't reach it, I won't think of you
as anything less than a force that could never be reckoned with.

Farewell, Eleanor.

Seventy-Three

Maisie's made it a habit to visit me
at least once a week with Caroline, but sometimes,
she has to reschedule because her life is in the river years.

Half the time, I'm too tired to hold a long conversation,
so it doesn't really matter anyway

and the best meals I eat are wrapped in plastic
before they lose all their texture in their microwave.

I could try baking like I used to, but the recipes are for a family of
two or more, so I try doing crosswords again

and feel a little bit clever before taking my
second nap since this morning and dreaming
of yesterday.

Seventy-Four

Joshua?

Seventy-Five

In the end, I cry.
Too old to have dreams, so hunger will do,
and so continues my eternal conflict with the pit.

Netted by the noises around me—what did you say?—
tangling me into confusion
with laughing lights from the TV entertained by my
extinguishable light,
a soul that's outlived its purpose,

and as I wail louder at the void I leave behind,
time is a breath between my cries and Maisie's
until warm arms like decades guide me to safety.
My mother's laughter.
Joshua singing.
Eleanor's smile.

There is hope in the darkness.

About the Author

Michelle Koubek earned her bachelor's degree in English Studies from The College of New Jersey in 2013. Her master's degree came several years later in special education from Grand Canyon University. She worked as an elementary teacher for several years in Hanahan, South Carolina before taking a leap and quitting to pursue her passion of writing. To this day, she believes educators deserve the utmost respect and appreciation. Some of the best women she knows have been teachers.

Her poetry and short stories have been published in over 25 publications including *Allegory, Ink Nest Poetry,* and *Strange Horizons.* She was diagnosed with autism as an adult and believes in increasing awareness among other females who may be undiagnosed. She is also a passionate visual artist and cannot get enough of board games and pizza. She lives in Florida now, filling her days with her passions and daydreaming about what tomorrow will bring.

www.ingramcontent.com/pod-product-compliance
Lightning Source LLC
Chambersburg PA
CBHW021328190426
43193CB00039B/446